I0813571
Like a Pro
Running
Curtis Duncan
AV2
www.openlightbox.com

Step 1
Go to **www.openlightbox.com**

Step 2
Enter this unique code
CLOKPSFK5

Step 3
Explore your interactive eBook!

AV2 is optimized for use on any device

Your interactive eBook comes with...

Audio
Listen to the entire book read aloud

Videos
Watch informative video clips

Weblinks
Gain additional information for research

Try This!
Complete activities and hands-on experiments

Key Words
Study vocabulary, and complete a matching word activity

Quizzes
Test your knowledge

Slideshows
View images and captions

Share
Share titles within your Learning Management System (LMS) or Library Circulation System

Citation
Create bibliographical references following the Chicago Manual of Style

This title is part of our AV2 digital subscription

1-Year K–5 Subscription
ISBN 978-1-7911-3320-7

Access hundreds of AV2 titles with our digital subscription.
Sign up for a FREE trial at **www.openlightbox/trial**

Contents

I love running. I am going for a run today.

People have been running for sport for hundreds of years.

I wear comfortable clothes and running shoes when I run.

Pro runners often wear tops called singlets.

Running shoes are the most important tools for runners.

Wearing the right shoes helps runners keep their feet safe.

People can run almost anywhere. I can run on paths or sidewalks.

Many running events are held on special tracks.

I warm up before I begin running. I stretch my legs and my back.

Pro runners often work with coaches who help them practice.

I run with my friends.
We like to race each other.

Pro runners may compete in long or short races.

I try to cross the finish line before anyone else. The first runner across the finish line wins the race.

Pro running events may use cameras at the finish line to help show who won.

Sometimes, I run on a relay team with my friends. We race against other teams.

Each runner on a team passes the baton to the next member of the team.

I love running.

RUNNING FACTS

These pages provide more detail about the interesting facts found in the book. They are intended to be used by adults as a learning support to help young readers round out their knowledge of each sport featured in the *Like a Pro* series.

Pages 4–5

Getting Ready Running is a sport and activity that has been around for as long as people have lived on Earth. Running as a sport can be traced back as far as 1829 BC in Ireland, where it was part of the Lughnasadh Festival. This closely resembled events from the Olympic Games that Greece began in 776 BC. In more modern times, there are records of amateur footraces being held in England in 1825 AD.

Pages 6–7

What I Wear Runners should wear clothes that do not impede their range of motion and shoes that will keep their feet protected. Injuries can occur very easily when running and sprinting. Many of these injuries are caused by issues with the training surface, the footwear, a lack of flexibility, a lack of strength, or improper running form.

Pages 8–9

What I Need Running shoes have cushioned areas in the heel and the forefoot. This helps the shoe handle the impact of the body's weight on the ground when a person is running. Some shoes also have a widened heel in order to provide stability. Running shoes are built to be flexible. An active runner may need to replace a pair of running shoes every four to six months.

Pages 10–11

Where I Play People can go running almost anywhere, including on roads, paths, trails, and tracks. Most dedicated running areas feature flat and safe surfaces for runners to race on in order to prevent injury. When running on trails or tracks, runners must navigate through the terrain as quickly as possible while doing their best to pace themselves based on the distance of the race or course they are running.

Pages 12–13

Warming Up Running can be both a leisure activity and a physically demanding one. It is extremely important to warm up before doing any kind of running. Warming up loosens muscles and reduces the chance of injury. A warm-up should include both stretching the muscle groups that will be used and some light activity. It is best to start a warm-up slowly and gradually build up the intensity toward the end.

Pages 14–15

Playing the Game Competitive running events are usually races. Races can range in distance from 328 feet (100 meters) to marathons of many miles (kilometers). The categories of races are determined by their distances. Anything equal to or less than 1,312 feet (400 m) in length is a sprint. Middle-distance running is anything between 2,625 and 9,843 feet (800 and 3,000 m). Long-distance running is anything beyond middle-distance running.

Pages 16–17

Winning the Game The first person to cross the finish line during a race wins the running event. Each runner must start at the same distance from the finish line as the others to ensure it is a fair race. If a race is close, some runners have been known to use a "finishing kick" at the end of a race. This is a burst of speed meant to push a runner over the finish line. Along with speed, both endurance and pacing are needed in order to win races.

Pages 18–19

Team Running The relay method of running was invented in the United States in 1883. A relay team has four people who must each run one quarter of the total distance of the race. The race begins with the first runner carrying a baton, which must be passed to the next runner on the team. The first team to complete the full length of the race with the baton wins.

Pages 20–21

I Love Running Running is a fun sport that can be enjoyed by almost anyone. It helps people stay active and healthy and is excellent for cardiovascular health. While running is good for overall health, it is also important for runners to eat healthy foods, such as fruits, vegetables, and grains. This will give the body the energy it needs to perform its best.

KEY WORDS

Research has shown that as much as 65 percent of all written material published in English is made up of 300 words. These 300 words cannot be taught using pictures or learned by sounding them out. They must be recognized by sight. This book contains 52 common sight words to help young readers improve their reading fluency and comprehension. This book also teaches young readers several important content words, such as proper nouns. These words are paired with pictures to aid in learning and improve understanding.

Page	Sight Words First Appearance
4	a, am, for, I, run
5	been, have, like, of, people, years
6	and, when
7	often
8	are, important, most, the
9	feet, helps, keep, right, their
10	almost, can, on, or
11	many
12	back, begin, before, my, up
13	them, who, with, work
14	each, other, to, we
15	in, long, may
16	first, line, try
17	at, show, use
18	sometimes
19	next

Page	Content Words First Appearance
5	pro, sport
6	clothes, running shoes
7	runners, singlets, tops
8	tools
10	paths, sidewalks
11	events, tracks
12	legs
13	coaches
14	friends
15	races
16	finish line
17	cameras
18	relay team
19	baton, member

Published by Lightbox Learning Inc.
276 5th Avenue, Suite 704 #917
New York, NY 10001
Website: www.openlightbox.com

Library of Congress Control Number: 2022934150

ISBN 978-1-7911-4845-4 (hardcover)
ISBN 978-1-7911-4846-1 (softcover)
ISBN 978-1-7911-4847-8 (multi-user eBook)

042022
100921

Printed in Guangzhou, China
1 2 3 4 5 6 7 8 9 0 26 25 24 23 22

Project Coordinator: John Willis
Designer: Jean Faye Marie Rodriguez

The publisher acknowledges Alamy, Getty Images, and Shutterstock as its primary image suppliers for this title.